THOUGHT

PROVOKING REFLECTIONS

DURING A PANDEMIC

Transforming Your Thoughts Into Breakthroughs

By

Roneiko Henderson-Beasley, LCSW

I dedicate this book to my one and only, Wendell, my son, who has pushed me beyond my wildest expectation within life to be the absolute best I can be as a human being. Thank you for everything you have brought into my life and for showing me how to enjoy life and chill when required. You allowed me the ability to carry the title of mom, and I wear it with pride.

To my mother, Debra, who listened to every Thought-Provoking Tuesday via our daily long-distance phone calls no matter the time of day or night. You provided me with the courage to write with your non-candy-coating truth. Your undying support has inspired me to accelerate to be a more incredible version of myself daily.

Contents

ACKNOWLEDGMENT

---◆—◆—◆---

To my family, GCFBC family, delta specials, friends, mentors, coworkers, and clients that have inspired me along the course, thank you for your encouragement, confirmation, and open dialog, and for allowing me to be a part of your journey within this path of life.

INTRODUCTION

While relaxing in my apartment, staring out the window, envisioning a prolific means to correspond with the families I served as the clinician in Busan, South Korean, I concluded upon incorporating a weekly social media blog during the early onset of the 2020 Pandemic.

The social media approach was to encourage people to reflect upon their thoughts as they embrace a new way of life for the world within which we live. I called the postings Thought Provoking Tuesday.

These messages I created were combined discussions with individuals, groups, and some personal experiences throughout the years. It was important these messages represented my truth and allowed individuals to connect and ponder their truth within as we as Americans experienced a worldwide Pandemic overseas.

Experiencing this Pandemic abroad was an authentic eye-opener. It allowed me to visit all my well-being components (physically, mentally, spiritually, emotionally), establishing what was important for me and my happiness. I embarked upon several personal transitions and transformations along the journey with the push of some endurance from a few underlining systematic racisms of privilege and entitlement. The obstacles generated significant discomfort; however, they empowered me to flourish as an individual and take a stand for me and my voice both personally and professionally.

As you read the provoking thoughts, I have provided self-reflection pages for the opportunity for you to record your thoughts and feelings as they may come upon reception of the message provided. Consider the changes within our world, then reminiscence on the world we once knew. What are your thoughts, and how did you grow, and are you growing from this Pandemic? There is always a time, reason, and season for each transition and transformation within our lives. What are you doing to make the changes you require to enjoy this life given to the fullest without regrets?

"Let us therefore make every effort to do what leads to peace and to mutual edification."

Romans 14:19 NIV

YOU ARE YOUR THOUGHTS

As we look outside our windows and see the not-so-busy streets, highways, bridges, and sidewalks, let's take a moment to reflect upon what we can do to ensure that we are taking care of ourselves during this time filled with uncertainties. We live in a world that has become so accustomed to the McDonaldization of society that we are now trying to assimilate a calmer, less hectic lifestyle we dreamed, talked, DM, IG, and even texted about relishing. However, many find it somewhat challenging to adjust to this new lifestyle implanted upon each of us.

How do we implement this new lifestyle forced upon us by COVID-19? Yes, we are experiencing a pandemic that has taken the world by shock, causing additional stress and worries upon the multitude. However, examine the situation from the perspective of a silver lining within, there is perhaps an opportunity to take advantage of the moments provided to spend with your loved ones.

When you reminisce upon those days filled with stress, insufficient time to complete tasks, what were you in search of in which you sought peace and tranquility in your life? Did it involve having more time to spend with those that you love? What role did your thoughts play in association with the stress clouding your day? How can you bring forth that sense of calm into your situation without allowing the distraction of the clutter returning to what you wanted to escape and will enable you to take control of your thoughts once again?

Positive thoughts provide us with better-coping skills during times of stress. Take a few moments today and reflect upon some positive thoughts to get you through this day.

"You are your thoughts, and your happiness lives within you."

Reflections, Thoughts, Breakthroughs

OBSTACLES AND ADVERSITIES

I recently had a student I taught a few years ago give me an update on his progression toward life in general. This formal student apprised me that although COVID 19 has put an early end to his last semester of college, he would be receiving his master's degree in social work in May. He wanted to thank me for encouraging him to continue his education, despite the odds stacked against him so many years prior. This formal student was a survivor of the Japan tsunami and had found himself homeless upon returning to the United States. He spoke openly about his thoughts and feelings regarding the unknowns associated with the Pandemic. He reminded me amid obstacles and adversities confronting us daily, we have two choices. We can allow them to control us, or we can take control. We both laughed because I had quoted those exact words to him several years ago when he was having a "feel sorry for himself type of day."

Life will bring forth many obstacles and misfortunes during our time, some good and some bad, but how you handle them makes the difference. When you face hardships and anxiety, where do you seek your strength? There has been a time when you thought an obstacle confronting you had defeated your attempt, be it an exam, physical, job interview, or finances, but you succeeded and came through.

Take a moment to reflect upon some previous obstacle or adversity you have overcome. Today, I inspire you to look for that same strength and know that you have that strength you are inquiring about, and it is more influential than ever. Trust and believe; you made it through the last obstacle and adversity, and you will make it through this one.

"Growth comes from our obstacles and adversities."

Reflections, Thoughts, Breakthroughs

COMMUNICATING THE ADJUSTMENTS

As we continue to adapt to our modern-day new normal, struggles continue to exist. What defines normal in this new way of life, which is changing daily? Many of us are creators of habit and like to stay true to our routine. However, our ability to adhere to flexibility and deviation is highly important in current times.

Adjusting to change and being flexible does not and will not look the same for everyone. The rearrangement of schedules, vacation plans placed on hold, virtual schooling, and postponed weddings are a few examples of changes in our world as we try to figure out the ins and outs of the Worldwide Pandemic.

As you go throughout your day, remember to follow up with your spouse, children, family members, and friends to see how they are adjusting to the new modifications injected into their schedules. Don't forget to do a self-check-in; how are you feeling with the recent changes?

Implementing these new changes can invoke mixed thoughts, feelings, and emotions. It is vital to express yourself with your loved ones. Make time during the day to verbalize your thoughts, feelings, and perceptions to avoid any misinterpretation.

"There is power in communicating."

Reflections, Thoughts, Breakthroughs

QUARANTINE PLAYLIST

I was perusing Spotify to explore the current release of music selection, considering what the general music-loving population worldwide is listening to. To my astonishment, there were several genres of Quarantine playlists provided during my search.

I was thrilled to see the assortment presented since music has been a go-to source of motivation and inspiration since I can recall. There is something about hearing lyrics of reassurance to stimulate you.

We all have something or someone that motivates and/or encourages us. Abraham Maslow's hierarchy of needs theory states that people are motivated by five categories of needs: physiological, safety, love, esteem, and self-actualization. This psychological theory allows us to distinguish what we need and what drives us.

When we examine the categories of needs outlined by Maslow, we regard our sense of motivation to attain. Individually, we can list needs, wants, and drives that spark our ability to achieve. What is your motivational force today? What will it take to inspire you to reach a lingering goal?

"Sometimes, the melody and lyrics of a song can provide the inspiration you require for the day."

Reflections, Thoughts, Breakthroughs

SMILE VS. FROWN

How many muscles are required to smile or frown? This is an interesting conversational topic for scientists and those that like to debate for decades. I have noticed along my travels that smiling is a generally reciprocated gesture.

How hard is it to construct a smile upon your face? I know many are thinking, what do I have to smile about during a time such as this? We have a lot to smile about, believe it or not. We have access to all human physiological needs: food, health, water, sleep, clothing, and shelter. A statement that may sound somewhat minimalistic; however, many individuals are not as fortunate to say they have these treasures.

It is easy to get into a grimace state of mind using several facial muscles when life circumstances have not explicitly permitted as we had planned. As learned with experience, there can always be interference inside a plan. We can sit around with either a frown or a smile. It is your choice. As you go throughout your day, allow your smile to deliver. It only takes a few muscles to achieve such a great feeling, and I am convinced that you may even feel a little laughter within your heart by doing so.

"A smile can brighten even the murkiest day."

Reflections, Thoughts, Breakthroughs

LET'S STAND TOGETHER

"Stand Together" is a recent slogan I have heard and seen during the pandemic, on podcasts, social media, and news outlets. When I see and hear the words, I ponder upon the representation and meaning of this slogan. We live in a world that admires TV personalities, sports superstars, and musical performers.

As I sit and catch up on one of my favorite DIY television programs, I am in awe of the breakout commercial, revealing a few of the network's TV personalities' rendering words of inspiration and encouragement to their fans from the privacy of their homes during this time of quarantine.

The opportunity to observe TV celebrities on a different platform with their spouses, significant others, children, and pets provides viewers with a glimpse of transparency and authenticity amongst individuals considered restricted in their everyday world. Yes, we live in a world where people come from all walks of life, and no, we all probably will not be on a weekly TV show. However, we all share a common denominator; we are humans. As humans, we should come together to support our fellow brothers and sisters in these demanding times. Division solves nothing besides mathematical and statistical equations. Our demands are individualized and specific; however, our ability to support is unified. Let's Stand Together today and always.

"Coming together, stand together, and see what we can accomplish together."

Reflections, Thoughts, Breakthroughs

THE SELF

As we watch the days become picturesque right before our eyes, what are your thoughts? Are you dreaming about what you could be doing if you were not confined to the restrictions caused by quarantine? If given the opportunity, we could spend countless hours reminiscing on the would've, could've, or should've done.

We each have an opportunity for self-reflection. Self-reflection analyzes one's thoughts, feelings, and behaviors for personal growth. Now, we aren't looking to criticize ourselves for not completing specific goals or projects, but it's time to look at who you would like to become. Let's describe it as a prioritization look at self-awareness.

When we look at our awareness of self, we examine our character and behavior and explore the changes we need to make. This new slow-paced normality of life can have its advantages when you look at it from a self-care perspective. Have you taken full advantage of the presented opportunities provided? I recently read an article providing the names of several universities that offer free college courses—what a great time to explore returning to school if that is your pleasure. It is also an opportune time to explore a new hobby or interest.

We encourage, inspire, and support family and friends regularly; however, we need to take that same level of enthusiasm and invest in ourselves. Take time to explore and expand upon your thoughts on what you need about the self.

"Self-reflection, self-awareness, self-care is both internal and external

growth."

Reflections, Thoughts, Breakthroughs

FEELINGS

Using our words and actions comes into play a lot more than we can count throughout the day. We answer phone calls, texts, emails, post on social media, and answer questions without second-guessing, utilizing verbal and nonverbal communications. Is there consideration taking into account your words' tone and the actions in which you are conveying your words?

We live in a society that dictates how and what we should feel. Growing up, I recollect when someone would speak sternly, one would say, "my feelings are hurt." Being penalized for expressing our feelings if they are not following what is proceeding at the time.

Webster's dictionary describes the word "feeling" as an emotional state or reaction. Throughout this time of adjusting, there are many spectrums of emotions. When you go to the doctor's office in pain, they ask you to rate your pain base on the emojis face pain chart. Often, people will give false information on these charts in fear of what they think will be thought of them based on their reveal.

The word "resilient" identifies an individual who can transform, adjust, and bounce back continually. We all will have our moment to be resilient; however, please take a few moments and examine your awareness in association with your feelings, honestly. Set in those feelings and accept that your feelings are important. Then determine how you want to address those feelings.

"Give yourself permission to be in your feelings."

Reflections, Thoughts, Breakthroughs

VISION BOARD

I was recently listening to a podcast and experienced a eureka moment. The message took me back to the beginning of the year, reminding me of my "Vision Board" preparation. I reminisce compiling the specific photos and motivational words to complete the board, which equated to the goals and aspirations I would complete for the year.

What affirmations and visual inspirations would catch my eye as I glance at this board throughout the year? Throughout the preparation for this board, there were no immediate thoughts of detours. Perhaps a few delays at the most; however, I would meet my attainment.

As a psychotherapist, I encourage my clients throughout their attainment. I motivate them to speak words of inspiration and encouragement to themselves and to pick themselves up if they stumble, preparing them for the trials and errors along the journey appropriately. Some individuals find it tricky, giving themselves value for their successes. However, they are quick to condemn themselves for their shortcomings. It is essential to nourish our consciousness. Let me suggest incorporating positive words of affirmations, inspiration, and motivation before starting your day and ending your day. You are so worthy and outstanding.

"Daily affirmations to self are inspiring."

Reflections, Thoughts, Breakthroughs

NORMS, BELIEFS, AND VALUES

As I prepare to watch my baby bird leave the nest and soar like an eagle, I reflect upon the journey he has ahead. The glasses he wears to see the world will be those of different lenses. What panoramic views will the world experience as we prepare as a collective society to return to a "new normal?"

Over the past few weeks, through social media, news broadcasts, and other outlets, the world's divided viewpoint has been front and center. We have witnessed multiples levels of tragedies related to the division amongst an ununited world.

As a multicultural world filled with individual norms, beliefs, and values, we have established and defined our additional subset classifications of normal. Just as we chartered and unified collectively to create our societal and individualized normality standards, we are now in search to fulfill the unknown. Many are calling this unknown the "new normal." We have subconsciously glimpsed this new standard and understand that it will take some adjusting, reintegration, and compliance.

We have proven our perseverance during a time of uncertainty. Let's continue to fight the fight, stand in unity, and remain encouraged. There must be better days ahead; I trust and believe in a great future for my son and the other sons and daughters stepping out into their future.

"Let's see it through together."

Reflections, Thoughts, Breakthroughs

DANCING

There has been this recent trend of attending virtual parties with the new stay at home lifestyle. Famous DJs are hosting daily and weekly Instagram parties, allowing the world an opportunity to come together through music. When I think of music, I immediately think of dancing because, in my subconscious, they go hand in hand. Dancing is something that I enjoy doing, even alone. There is something about connecting with the beat that gets me moving, puts a smile on my face and warms up my heart.

Psychologists have reported that dancing is good for both the body and mind. When I think about dancing over the years by myself, competitively, and with others from all over the world, the definition that dancing is universal rings true. We each dance to the beat of our drum; however, those individual beats come together collectively as we share the art of dancing with others.

Our society allows us to utilize the arts and creativity to assist us in times of trouble outside of simple talk therapy to address our thoughts, feelings, and behaviors through art therapy and dance movement therapy. Dance movement therapy is also known as movement psychotherapy, which is associated with the reduction of stress. I think we all can take full advantage of some stress reduction with a few dance moves. Put on those dancing shoes, and let's go. Your mind, body, and soul deserve it.

"Dancing to the beat of your drum."

Reflections, Thoughts, Breakthroughs

SOCIOLOGY THE FAMILY

I recently had an opportunity to catch up with a mentor. It was great to hear from him. He taught me so much as I embarked upon my journey teaching Sociology, which seems to happen a lifetime ago. The conversation switched gears as we both reflect upon our gratitude after exchanging pleasantries. We experience life from two generations and perspectives yet share mutual respect, empathy, and compassion for individuals and families worldwide that have been traumatized through this crisis.

The 2020 pandemic has enabled families to visit the compositional meaning of their family. We each have our unique representation of the family. I have added individuals over the years to my family because they represent themselves as such.

The family's social institution and how it begins and evolves is the concept of the Sociology Family class I taught several years ago. With time comes change as with life, significant or not, so good.

Each day, we have 24 hours of opportunities. We take so much for granted daily, the essentials. Have you expressed your gratitude to those within your social unit, defined as your family? There are 1440 minutes furnished per day. Please take a few of those minutes to tell those you call family how much they mean to you.

"Family is family; you pick up extra members along the way."

Reflections, Thoughts, Breakthroughs

TWENTY-ONE DAYS

Over the past few months, there has been a complete transformation worldwide. The old cliché that "it takes all kinds of people to make a world go around" has been insightful. I have had the opportunity to converse and observe family, friends, associates, students, clients, and a few individuals without a category. Exploring the hearts of humanity within our world is befitting during this time. We all have our individual opinions, perspectives, and insights over numerous subjects within life in general. However, what do we do when there is a heart change within these opinions, stances, or doctrines? It takes twenty-one days to create a new habit or break an old one.

Interestingly, creating change requires a new behavioral thought process per the stages of change. We can go back and forth between contemplation and maintaining the change we seek individually or collectively. Change is inevitable; however, we vocalize that we want modification in our growth, but are we willing to do the work for the change we require in our life? We are not ready, getting ready, or already ready with this change. Where do you fall within the stages of change for what you are seeking in life?

"A change of heart can be healing."

Reflections, Thoughts, Breakthroughs

GREAT

As a child, I recollect the excitement of hearing that the "Greatest Show" on Earth was coming to a city near you. That was the slogan for Barnum & Bailey Circus. Not sure what the meaning of the "Greatest Show" on Earth meant as a young child, but it sounded so powerful and filled with prestige through the radio commentator. Barnum & Bailey understood how to market children of all ages with such a power-filled trademark. They indeed provided you with eye-catching performances throughout the show if you could attend their circus.

We all have our individualized interpretation of that magical word "great." There is a preoccupation with attaching suffixes to the name for its meaning to be enlarged. The life drawn from a rainbow of simplicity to complexity is what we experience from childhood to adulthood. Be it simplistic or sophisticated, there is a continuous search for high excellence with all objectives identified.

We get so lost in the requests set upon us that we neglect to create time to enjoy the simplicity of life we encountered in our youth. Let's take that magical word "great" and convert it to grateful and gracious for making it to this current moment in time, even amid the demands of life.

"Celebrate you; you are great in all that you do."

Reflections, Thoughts, Breakthroughs

CHARACTER OF COMMUNICATION

Living in a world filled with various expression forms, we utilized several outlets to communicate our thoughts, feelings, and behaviors. Often, without considering the impact that our delivery will have on those on the receiving end. Properly known as the act of "react verse response." Your choice; some argue that they are the same. However, I suppose they feel significantly different upon receipt.

When we communicate, be it verbal or nonverbal, it speaks volumes to your character. What are you conveying when you talk to people daily? What are they thinking upon retrieval? If I asked three individuals about your style of communication towards them, how would they respond? Would I gather the same information from everyone? Do you find your communication exchange and/or style changing depending upon your environment?

We all strive to be assertive communicators, standing up for not only ourselves but for the rights of others. Getting your point across effectively can occur without insulting, sabotaging, hurting, telling untruths, degrading, and alienating others. Although assertive communication is the ideal form of communication, studies have shown that most individuals fall short of reaching this goal.

I have discovered that individuals are becoming more aggressive in their communication, both personally and professionally. They are leaving people feeling vulnerable through insults of words, which equates to being bullied.

I encourage you to observe your communication style and make the necessary adjustments to fit the character you are displaying and communicating publicly to represent the legacy you would like to leave.

"Your communication represents more than you think."

Reflections, Thoughts, Breakthroughs

MASK LIFE

---◆◆◆---

I just received news that another close friend has been diagnosed as a victim of COVID-19. I don't know how to feel as the stories are becoming more frequent. Following all mandates established and taking extra precautions to assure that his family remains free from the virus. I needed to hear my friend's voice, so I reached out via Skype to check-in.

My friend described his depression upon notification of the positive results and a sense of anger towards the COVID-19 virus. He reported in his state that many individuals are refusing to wear masks. Reporting feeling that it's against their constitutional right to be forced to wear something against their will. I could feel his frustration through the telephone thousands of miles away. I immediately pondered the protocols and mandates established that have kept my son and me safe while living abroad during this Pandemic.

I was grateful that my friend was still alive to address his concerns regarding the virus but saddened by current losses in the virus's expanse After completing our brief conversation due to my friend's inability to breathe and talk simultaneously, I experienced a deep sense of empathy for all the families affected by this crisis.

"No one is immune; let's remain as safe as possible."

THE MIRROR

———◆◆◆———

Do you like what you see when you examine yourself in the mirror? Many individuals cannot gaze into the mirror for longer than five minutes without noticing their own flaws. We make correlations with marketed advertisement platforms on what we should mimic. We are all created to look a certain way uniquely diverse for a reason; theoretically, scientifically, we can debate that justification. However, what would happen if everyone did a deep self-exploration? Would you like the results that would surface?

We all can reflect on the things in life we would like to change if we could. With modern technology, we can significantly change our outer appearances if we please, without even lifting one finger. We spend tons of money yearly to make outward impressions and improvements to ourselves. However, we rarely talk to our friends or family about investing time or money on self-improvements or self-awareness.

I implore you to take time and invest in yourself as it relates to the wellbeing of your character and your inner presence. The results will prove one of your best investments if you are open to truth and honesty. The transparency to oneself will be the most astonishing transformation, theoretically and scientifically.

"Liking what you see is up to you."

CHANGE AGENTS

I recently had the opportunity to sit down with some phenomenal ladies to speak very openly about the dynamics of world issues, just woman to woman. The group included women from all social, ethnic, educational, spiritual, and economic backgrounds. We defined the outcome we wanted to achieve through our conversation, not making any attempts to overlook individual experiences or beliefs. We spoke, appreciating being heard with no reservations, and listened attentively with open hearts earnestly, wanting to acquire something that we could transmit back to console our fellow sister. We each communicated that change is what we needed to discern within the world where we reside.

It's interesting how instantly people can commit to a demand to see the change yet make no effort to make the change needed both inwardly and outwardly. There are ample opportunities provided to emendations to systematic historical errors and rectify disagreements in association with the present bias. Life is concise; when it comes down to it, to allow your conceit to come into taking a stand for what is right. On that day, we each committed to one another and the individual self we would stand for what was right and become the change-agents that the world requires.

"Committed to making a difference, through actions, not just words."

Reflections, Thoughts, Breakthroughs

SOCIAL WORK

I recently had a long in-depth conversation with an endeared coworker that I worked with over twenty-five years ago regarding our ability to help others transform their lives as social workers. We reminisced on the foundational concepts of social work and why we entered the field. Although many years have passed, our passion and mission remain strong. Once young social workers, green in the arena on the streets of New Orleans, learning how to navigate the policies and procedures to be all we could be for our clients. Little did we know that we were outlining transformational lifestyles for those whose lives we entered with their help.

I learned a lot about people during those early days as a social worker; even more about myself as an advocate and a human. There will come a time in each of our lives where we will have an opportunity to provide a glimpse of hope, an inspirational or encouraging word to a family member, friend, coworker, or even a stranger. Are you ready to make a difference in transforming someone's day by providing that smile, encouraging word, or a listening ear? Perhaps, the lending of a few bucks, a blanket, or a community resource. It doesn't require you to be a board-certified clinician; the only requirement is to be in tune with a fellow human's need.

"Your simple act of kindness can be a motivating factor in someone's life."

Reflections, Thoughts, Breakthroughs

CURVEBALL

Life has a way of throwing around many curveballs, both expected and unexpected. However, what I have learned through the years is how you discern those expected and unexpected moments of life is when the ball game starts.

Baseball has never been a sport I have been very fond of watching or attending. However, I must admit that I had a heart change upon attending my first game in Seoul a few years back. The enthusiasm provided at the match was beyond words and exceeded the expectations of myself and my coworkers. We came to the game expecting to witness a regular match between two opposing teams with nine endings, popcorn, hot dogs, beer, and cheering. Unexpected was a time of fellowship with strangers, embracing a culture, and celebrating a known sport worldwide without language barriers being an issue. That evening, eight clinicians from various parts of the United States discovered that although we had only been in Korea for less than 72 hours, we felt a part of a culture, unexpectedly, through a sporting event that has been around for ages. The curveball we received that night was an insight into the world we would live in over the next year; what a great throw.

"The happenings of life at a sporting event will surprise you."

4 ELEMENTS OF HEALTH

As I traveled back to the states to prepare my son for his next journey in life, there were many different perspectives I pondered as I watched people from all walks of life come and go throughout the airport. I witnessed individuals wearing full-body protective coverings to individuals not even wearing a mask properly.

We are living within a Pandemic that has affected everyone in some shape or form. Within the current juncture, we must decide to better our physical, emotional, mental, and spiritual health. Within these decisions of betterment, there are the confines of culture. The subject of culture isn't being addressed but avoided due to the ongoing denial of division. Many of us fall short of assuring that our physical, emotional, mental, and spiritual health is intact, even in the best of times. So, what can we do to make sure that we appropriately adhere to these elements during a crisis?

Incorporating a daily self-check-in on how you feel from head to toe would help address these four elements. How are you genuinely adjusting to the current normal? What can you do with handling the arenas within that are lacking? These are questions you can ask for soliciting and identifying clarity. Life as we once knew it is non-absolute; therefore, we must continue to adjust and fine-tune daily. Individually, we all will have a different plan of action that must be taken; however, collectively, we all share the same program to complete the plan.

"Finding our balance within to assure and align our outer peace."

Reflections, Thoughts, Breakthroughs

PUZZLES

I recall as a child watching my mother complete puzzles, crosswords, seek-a-word and picture. I thought, "what a tedious task to partake upon;" there appeared to be no fun or pleasure. Little did I know, I would come to recognize the joy, peace, calm, and serenity of those puzzles brought to a mother of four at the end of a day filled with many barriers, hardships, and tasks.

Today we live in a society that requires us to be experts in multi-tasking. As we seek to discern multitasking fully, we need dedicated time to cultivate a reduction of stress within all areas of our being. We have navigated from the simplicity of life due to society's overly stimulated demands on keeping up with social media's ins and outs. These demands have allowed many individuals to lose sight of what once represented joy, peace, calm, and serenity.

As I sit and watch my mother over fifty years later enjoying doing her puzzles, not on a smartphone, but with a pen and paper, in silence with no care in the world, I smile. I am thankful to have grown up to witness the importance of finding your joy, peace, calm, and serenity, even amongst the simplicity, as I complete my puzzle right beside her.

"Enjoying and appreciating the simple things of life."

FORGIVENESS

I was recently watching a movie where a mother explained to her young children the importance of forgiving those that may have hurt your feelings, embarrassed you, or were merely rude for no reason. I thought, what if it was that easy for adults to buy into the synopsis this mother provided to her children?

Forgiveness is a word that contains an abundance of power in the world we dwell in. However, we live in a society that solicits the opposite. Consumption of both afflictions and inflictions has individuals conflicted. How do you forgive, and are you willing to forgive those that have incurred affliction and infliction?

Over the years, I have met many individuals encountering difficulties forgiving people who have brought distress upon them and forgiving themselves for their inflictions upon themselves.

It takes courage to find genuine forgiveness towards individuals that have brought continuous hurt or pain. However, it takes tremendous bravery to forgive thyself for infliction subjected both intentionally and unintentionally.

Today, I employ you to establish a moment of forgiveness, not only to those who may have brought unnecessary burdens but forgive yourself of any shortcomings you feel you may have brought upon yourself.

"Let it go and see how great you feel."

Reflections, Thoughts, Breakthroughs

CROSSING OUR PATHS

Throughout this journey in life, I have discovered that many people will enter our life path. Each will have their time, reason, and season for treading into our path, either abruptly, unexpectedly, or intentionally. Yes, we have our family we are born into and the ones we inherit through marriage or lifetime friendships. However, how do we describe those individuals who enter our path and leave such an impressionable mark we cannot justify or define their timing, reason, or season for entering our lives?

A dear friend once told me that timing is of the essence, and when it is precise and in order, all will fall right into place. However, we are living in a world that cannot be predicted by time or timing. We all have a very descriptive definition behind our individualized logic or reason. I heard some describe it as the luck of the draw.

My favorite is the season behind it all. We know that we are given four seasons throughout the year. I always encourage individuals to re-evaluate themselves during each season, executing the changes needed, winter, spring, summer, and fall. We have our likes and dislike in association with each season presented; however, we will go about our lives and live within each season, enduring what cometh from within that season.

Consider an individual placed into your life path, disregard the time limit of their specific presence, ponder upon the time, reason, and season for their entrance. It's amazing how the timing is precise and perfect, the cause/reason specifically on point, and the season was within the moment needed. When all is said, that is all that matters.

"There's intent within the timing, reason, and season for each moment we encounter."

Reflections, Thoughts, Breakthroughs

RELEASING

As I reflect on the impediments I have overcome, I recall how significant it is to release. Releasing is such a powerful tool-very intentional, yet many hold on to rancor and miss out on the fundamental freedom they will gain by merely releasing those that have brought persecution against them in some form. I know that it is easier said than done often, and I had to learn how to permit myself to release sincerely. Some torments and pains form deep and shatter within that require more extended time to heal than others.

I have heard some say they can forgive but not forget or forget and not forgive. To own real peace within, I have discovered that total forgiveness is required. We all have induced hurt or pain upon someone, be it intentionally or unknowingly. Not surprisingly, we solicit forgiveness when we perpetrate against a fellow loved one, friend, or coworker. However, many find it challenging to examine that same forgiveness upon reciprocation. What justification have you allowed yourself to cling to, avoiding releasing someone? Find internal and external peace with the removal of those justifications.

"Releasing equates to inner peace."

TECHNOLOGY

When was the last time you unplugged? I know you are perhaps thinking, "what is she referring to when she says unplug?" I mean shutting everything down and returning to the basics. Can you go without using technology for two hours or even an entire twenty-four hours? I know this task may be more challenging for some than others, but in a world so driven by technology, have you considered how relaxing it could be to avoid the constant stress associated with our technologically filled world.

As a clinician, I have seen more people associating their anxiety and stress with the demands of keeping up with technology. Many compare their achievements of life via social media and postings.

I remember the days when the TV signed off at midnight, we had only five channels to watch, and we were content with exploring our unlimited options outside of the black and white television in our living room. In today's world, we have become so accustomed to technology that many cannot cope without having immediate access.

I have noticed that restaurants offer their WIFI codes to their patrons to keep them occupied both stateside and aboard. I watch couples and families sit at tables without conversing with one another, however fully engaged in with their electronic devices.

The Pandemic has allowed ample opportunity for families to reunite. However, I have witnessed families becoming even more isolated due to the constant need for technology.

Returning to old fashion basics, let's do an individualized experiment and see how long you can go without using your cell phone, tablet, or computer and commit to genuine communication exchange or exploring a new hobby.

"Once upon a time, we did just fine without them all."

OPEN TO CHANGE

I have heard on more than one occasion throughout my lifespan that change is inevitable. It is a true statement; however, we occasionally defy evolution in most cases as humans. We like to stick to what we know and stay within the circumscribed known stability verse taking a risk toward change.

After speaking with individuals regarding the changes they have had to make to sustain the climate within our world, one thing holds, life is very precious, and this is not the time to stress the small hiccups presented. What is essential and does it matter, are the questions I have presented to clients as it correlates to their individualized inflicted changes.

After visiting the questions, many have a change of heart regarding their initial position on transition. We are over three-fourths through this year, and we must incorporate daily change within our schedules. Change can equate to growth, healing, and surviving when comparing to the thoughts and perspectives presented. I believe we all can benefit from growth, healing, and new surviving techniques—the incorporation of change has a new meaning for each of us.

"What is your new equation for change?"

Reflections, Thoughts, Breakthroughs

LESSON WITHIN THE SEASON

As I glance out the window and observe another season change, I am in awe of how quickly the seasons come and go. I recently had the opportunity to catch up with a dear friend. We have been conversing and providing one another with emotional and spiritual support for over twenty years. We agree that the new season approaching brings forth mixed feelings and emotions. There have been numerous modifications with the new season. These modifications have embodied uncertainties and enthusiasm with what we must look forward to during upcoming seasons—personal and professional growth.

During our conversation, it dawned upon me that we not only need accountability partners to exist within our inner circle, but we also need personal cheerleaders to cheer us on when we no longer have the energy to do so ourselves. Over the years, I have shared my inspirations, failures, and plans with a few individuals I thought held my best interest at heart, only to discover otherwise. However, I did not allow those moments to deter my path.

With life come many lessons, and through lessons comes growth. What have your life lessons taught you, and can you identify your growth through those lessons? Answering these questions doesn't imply that you need to go down a dark memory lane and identify or relive your defeats but recognize what you acquired from those lessons presented. Those lessons of growth are unswerving signs you are no longer the individual you once were, but a new individual closer to those personal and professional goals you have established.

"Life lessons delays signify a winning season."

Reflections, Thoughts, Breakthroughs

YOUR TRUTH

Upon my return to the United States, there has been an influx of life-coaching referrals. When the requests come in, I am always interested in exactly what type of life coaching individuals employ in soliciting. We live in a world filled with many professionals to help individuals work through various issues or obstacles confronting them. Many individuals are searching for instant gratification to avoid dealing with life in general—avoiding the truth.

There is a lot of truth avoiding today due to individuals living in a fictional world. People have begun to believe the untruths they tell themselves and others daily. They seek approval through social media outlets, material purchases, and unhealthy relationships for the status quo. When they reach my office for assistance, many are only beseeching how they can keep up the current images they are portraying. Many are unaware of their truth any longer due to their long history of portrayal to keep up a false image to impress people who do not care.

So, I ask, why are you exerting some energy to present a façade that has you miserable? People will treat you how you allow them to treat you. That includes self. Isn't it time to have a little more respect for yourself and stop worrying about what other people think or say?

"Living in your truth is the real coaching of life."

BIRTHDAY CELEBRATION

I had an opportunity to participate in my first honk-and-wave birthday celebration recently. It was great seeing everyone that showed up to display their love to the birthday girl celebrating her 70th. We drove down the street with balloons and signs on our cars, blowing our horns in honor of her. Who would have ever known this would be the new way to celebrate the ones we love on their born day? I must admit that the Pandemic has sparked the Corpus Callosum of our brain. The level of creativity displayed to celebrate monumental occasions has been phenomenal.

A few days after celebrating my dear friend's special day, I pondered my creativity developed during this Pandemic and how I would celebrate my birthday approaching. I will miss the opportunity to receive my yearly two-hour massage; however, this will need to be placed on hold until there is some control over this COVID-19. However, I took the opportunity to reflect, relate, and release as it correlates to my creative transformation developed or inspired to be concise.

As I reminisce over 365 days around the sun celebrating another year of life, I am beyond grateful for every twist, pull, and tug associated with the transformation that has taken place and the continuation of its evolution. There have been a plethora of laughs and tears and in-betweens throughout this journey. I am ecstatic with the person I see in the mirror—looking forward to the continued extension that emerges from the numerous transitions of this life given.

"Happy Born Day, there is greater for the upcoming year."

DO YOU HEAR WHAT I HEAR?

As a psychotherapist, I aid individuals in association with conflict and anger management. One of the principal elements of the conflict and escalated anger has been ineffective communication exchange. Our expectations and projection within our communication exchange play an indispensable role in all areas of our life.

Our communication method is specifically critical; in all relationships, courtship, partnership, or friendship. Without effective communication, the relationship will have no substance. Utilizing accurate communication to convey your message and open communication to accept a message is exceptionally significant within the exchange.

Several years ago, I participated in a marriage retreat. It was intriguing to hear many describing miscommunications signals within the relationships between less than a year to over 70. It only takes a moment to inquire what is going on and reveal how you feel to avoid unnecessary tension, dismay, anger, rejection, and stress when exchanging dialog. I realize this concept may not be as straightforward as it sounds. However, when we revisit significant communication dialogues that may have got out of hand, we can acknowledge that asking a few questions could have eliminated some disheartenment. Many factors come into play when we communicate, and perhaps, we should view the entire scenario before responding, including our hearts.

"There is more to communicating than meets the eyes and mouth."

Reflections, Thoughts, Breakthroughs

STEPPING OUT ON FAITH

Stepping out on faith is one of those declarations that I have heard many times, and I have referenced it myself on several occasions. I have feared stepping into unknowing faith due to the possible outcome of failure. I have faced many failed attempts, too many to account for at this moment. Each has revealed a teachable order along the way with some enhanced character building and thickening of the skin.

My brand-new outlook on failure has a uniquely defined perspective differing from my old linear perspective, which consisted of back-to-back delayed gratification wallowing—what a mouthful and what an emotional rollercoaster each teachable lesson allowed me to endure. It is cautiously to confess to those lessons learned now; however, I was in an unusual mindset through those teachable moments.

I wouldn't say that failure has become my companion. However, it allowed me to explore my internal and external flaws and genuinely seek and explore my domains needing development.

I have learned to trust and become in tune with my abilities and my higher power to step out on faith and know that all will be beyond okay and fall right into succession because what is for me is for me. Your faith will take you further than you will ever imagine in life.

"A failure can bring forth a successful lesson when you are open to seeing and believing."

COFFEE BREAK DISCUSSION

After getting lost in the hospital corridors, I had the opportunity to sit down over coffee with a stranger. After exchanging pleasantries, she spoke about having revelations in association with her friends and family's discovery. She recalled recently returning to the Hampton Roads areas, aspiring to be inundated by check-ins. I petitioned clarification; she declared that she wanted to believe they were happy to witness her return. However, she reported silence. I shared that I had recently returned to the area after being abroad and discovered while residing overseas that out of sight constitutes for some individuals as "not on my mind." Growing up, the adage was "out of sight, out of mind."

What I have learned about individuals is that when it is convenient, they will reach out. When I say convenient, it implies when there may be a need or a want, which you can supply for them. I have heard many use justifications regarding the Pandemic on why they aren't calling and checking up on their so-called family and friends; however, they are frequently on social media and stay up to date on the ins and outs of new videos and such. People find time to do what is essential to them and make time for important people.

During our coffee break conversation, I suggested that my new friend decide how important the individuals she had hoped to hear from meant to her and her life equation. She reported that she has reached out on several occasions and no follow through on the other end. We both laughed, although our eyes did not show laughter. She looked at me and replied that it hurts, but I must move on because I only continue to bring pain to myself if I don't.

"Moving in and out of lives brings forth mixed feelings with all parties involved."

HELLO AND GOODBYE

Each day we can chat, experience, compete, embrace, laugh and mourn our families, friends, strangers, and even individuals who may not have a given title along this journey of life. Despite the relationship exchange that has partaken, there comes a time that we must part and say goodbye or perhaps so long to the relationship. Several families affiliated with the military find themselves in this situation every 18 to 24 months due to a permanent change of station (PCS). Somewhat of a challenging assignment even when, sometimes, the departure may be a requirement for individual growth and healing when it is not associated with a work-related move.

Throughout this journey, we grow. Sometimes, growth may erupt a separation within a once-inseparable union. Providing reassurance through strength-based counseling when working with clients going through a separation or divorce has been rewarding. I have discovered that people like confirmation about their strengths when processing through healing verse constant recall of imperfections and blaming oneself.

Working from a strength base allows the opportunity to encourage individuals of their inner strength and resiliency. When you say goodbye to a relationship you invested your valuable time and energy, you can lose sight of your most valuable assets, yourselves. Take that inner strength and resilience and say hello to the new and improved you.

"A goodbye can translate to a new beginning for you."

Reflections, Thoughts, Breakthroughs

TO NEW BEGINNINGS

Life can sometimes provide you with a sense of compromise and contentment. We can get so comfortable with day-to-day life activities and forget that we deserve more than we are accepting. During this Pandemic, I have heard the reverberations of many, searching and longing for something different within as the world surrounding them has dismantled. However, what does or what would a new beginning consist of for many in searching?

I have surveyed many only through general conversation over the past few months to grasp what people seek regarding new inceptions or a fresh start. Receiving responses such as love, happiness, peace, independence, truth, wealth, health, and unity were among the top consensus.

In my consideration of the acknowledgments given, I deliberated on my awareness as I envision how I would describe a new beginning or fresh start according to the answers provided. I would yearn to have love, unconditionally, along with unshaken peace. Independence, though, with support through the unparallel truth. Wealth in a financial sight, along with my health, would be essential. Unity amongst them all would consummate and make it a firm and solid foundation.

If It were only that simple, some would say. It can be if you put your mind, heart, and soul into the new beginning or fresh start you desire. What is stopping you from starting anew and birthing that dream that thrives within? Go back to school, follow your heart, travel the world, say no, and be okay with that as your final answer. You deserve it all; never doubt yourself as you prepare for the next chapter of your life.

"The YOU in YOU believes in You."

Reflections, Thoughts, Breakthroughs

ZOOM ON RELATIONSHIPS

During a fun Zoom night, catch-up call with friends, the subject of relationships entered the zoom as many return to the dating scene after divorce. We all laughed because we knew it would be an intriguing conversation amongst friends over wine.

One friend shared that he had recently befriended a charming individual several months ago, who has him considering marriage. As they became acquainted, he reported being pleasantly surprised by all they had in common. It's interesting how music, television programming, food dishes, and even old sayings from your childhood can spark conversations of comfort.

Another friend chimed in and stated that she fell for a smooth-talker who spoke the language of love; however, his actions projected differently. She confided that she had been open with him regarding her feelings towards him after a few months, only to receive mixed feelings.

The collective advice given to our friends came with love. Sometimes being an open book, your authentic self when establishing a relationship, can bring about uncertainties for the other person. Those intricacies may involve past concerns in association to trust and love.

Secure the ground rules and communicate what you are seeking and require when entering a relational contract. Trust along with your heart of love are two exceptional attributes to bring to the table, only simultaneously when the feelings are mutual. Perhaps, the intention may not be per expanding upon a relationship but thoroughly enjoying the company of one another. It takes time to discover the truth behind the exchange of a relationship.

"Know your role before claiming a title in any relationship; it will eliminate hurt feelings and or a broken heart."

Reflections, Thoughts, Breakthroughs

I AM "GOOD"

Do you ever say that you are "good" or "okay" when people ask how you are doing? I guess it is just a standard response as I do not get many people who check in on me regularly because I am the go-to person who checks in with everyone else. I had to psychoanalyze my response when a friend brought to the attention that I announce that I am "good" often, but am I "good"?

Perhaps the prevailing life circumstances I am embarking upon triggered the question. I attempted to shift the word and say I am okay. However, it did not work on this day for this friend. So, what exactly is good and or okay in your book was the rhetorical question. I realized that I used them both to avoid addressing what I am going through because I have discovered that we live in a society that may ask how you are doing but don't want to hear how you are doing.

In my profession, I assist people to come up with solutions to their problems; therefore, I have generated a method of handling my circumstance to avoid overloading my friends. Over the years, I have mastered some great self-care strategies that provide the opportunity to relax and release. However, I have also discovered that it has been more accessible to address some life events with strangers. These conversations can be held doing training, over coffee, or even at a grocery store, because sometimes what you may speak may be what needs to be heard by the individual listening.

"All parties involved have a fulfilled need that's met, which makes it "good."

Made in the USA
Middletown, DE
02 April 2021

36763388R00073